Catholic Prayers & Devotions

Catholic Classics

Edited by

Rev. Victor Hoagland, C. P.

Illustrated by

William Luberoff

THE REGINA PRESS
New York

Nihil Obstat: Otto L. Garcia, J.C.D.
                    Diocesan Censor

Imprimatur: ✝ Francis J. Mugavero, D.D.
                    Bishop of Brooklyn, N.Y.

Date: November 24, 1981

Excerpted from
My Prayer Book © 1981, by Regina Press, New York

BRIEF STATEMENT OF CHRISTIAN DOCTRINE

The Core of Christian Faith

Yes, Jesus Christ is our Teacher and Lord. His life and words draw men and women of every age and nation to his side. No other great figure of history approaches what he said and did.

Born poor, his childhood spent in an obscure Galilaean village, he suddenly emerged for a few dazzling years to teach and work wonders in the Jewish world of his time.

He was opposed by those in power who brought him to trial and crucified him. After three days he rose from the dead.

Those who were witnesses to his Resurrection told the good news to others. They were convinced he was the Son of God who came to bring new life and hope to a world lost in darkness. He would bring a new kingdom, a new order, based on justice and love.

Jesus promised to remain always with his Church. Receiving the Holy Spirit, his Church would proclaim his life and words. Above all, they would offer the world his love.

The Sacraments

The Catholic Church seeks to remain one with Jesus Christ in a variety of ways. One of these is the sacraments — seven great signs that mark the different stages and events in human life. From birth till death, the follower of Jesus reaches out to him for power and life to love and live as he did. The sacraments are key events for Christ to draw men and women more fully into his saving actions. These ritual acts of human communication and human worship in the church are events of grace in which the Spirit of God is imparted by the Lord who is ever sending His Spirit into the world. Through the sacraments Jesus is always present to those who believe in him.

They are:

Baptism

Confirmation

Eucharist

Reconciliation

Anointing of the Sick

Matrimony

Holy Orders

The Beatitudes

Jesus promised happiness to those who believed in him and follow his teaching. He summed up his promises in his Sermon on the Mount. What he taught there, he lived himself and the stories and events of the New Testament re-echo these same central truths. The Beatitudes are a summary of the different directions in life that lead to the peace and happiness promised by Jesus. The traditional listing of the beatitudes is:

1. Blessed are the poor in spirit: the reign of God is theirs.

2. Blessed are the sorrowing: they shall be consoled.

3. Blessed are the lowly: they shall inherit the land.

4. Blessed are they who hunger and thirst for holiness: they shall have their fill.

5. Blessed are they who show mercy: mercy shall be theirs.

6. Blessed are the single-hearted: for they shall see God.

7. Blessed are the peacemakers: they shall be called sons of God.

8. Blessed are those persecuted for holiness' sake: the reign of God is theirs.

The Works of Mercy

Jesus told us to love one another as he loved us. His own life revealed his loving concern and compassion for the poor, the sick, and the troubled. The leper isolated from society, the blind man alone in his darkness, the frightened woman taken in adultery, the thief condemned to a cross found in him care, support, and strength. He advised those who would follow him to make their love as practical and selfless as his own. The corporal and spiritual works of mercy are guidelines for Christian love.

The Corporal Works of Mercy

To feed the hungry.
To give drink to the thirsty.
To clothe the naked.
To visit and ransom the captives.
To shelter the homeless.
To visit the sick.
To bury the dead.

The Spiritual Works of Mercy

To admonish sinners.
To instruct the ignorant.
To counsel the doubtful.
To comfort the sorrowful.
To bear wrongs patiently.
To forgive all injuries.
To pray for the living and the dead.

The Ten Commandments

Jesus reaffirmed the law that Moses, inspired by God, gave to the Jewish people. He came, he said, not to destroy the law but to fulfill it. Through the centuries the Judeo-Christian moral code has become a basic guideline for human conduct.

The human family left to its own wisdom often pursues a course of violence and destruction. The human heart, whose ways are "torturous" according to the Prophet Jeremiah, is prone to contraction and selfishness. "Out of the human heart comes evil thoughts, murder, adultery, fornication, theft, false witness, slander" (Mt. 15, 19).

The Ten Commandments warn of human deception and at the same time point out the proper way for one to live. Following Jesus Christ means to follow their teaching.

1. I, the Lord, am your God. You shall not have other gods besides me.

2. You shall not take the name of the Lord, your God, in vain.

3. Remember to keep holy the Sabbath Day.

4. Honor your father and your mother.

5. You shall not kill.

6. You shall not commit adultery.

7. You shall not steal.

8. You shall not bear false witness against your neighbor.

9. You shall not covet your neighbor's wife.

10. You shall not covet anything that belongs to your neighbor.

The Greatest Commandment of All

"But when the Pharisees heard that he had silenced the Sadducees they got together and, to disconcert him, one of them put a question, 'Master, which is the greatest commandment of the Law?' Jesus said, 'You must love the Lord your God with all your heart, with all your soul, and with all your mind. This is the greatest and the first commandment. The second resembles it: You must love your neighbor as yourself. On these two commandments hang the whole Law, and the Prophets also.'"

MATT. 22, 34-40

Ecclesiastical Laws

It is in Christ that authority of the Church dwells. The laws of the Church and the legitimate commands of the pope and bishops are issued with the authority Christ gave to the Church for the good of the People of God. The bishops of each country generally list the most notable of special duties of Catholics as "Precepts of the Church." The bishops of the United States have endorsed the following for their people. (Those traditionally mentioned as precepts of the Church are marked with an asterisk.)

1. To keep holy the day of the Lord's resurrection: to worship God by participating in Mass every Sunday and Holy Day of Obligation: * to avoid those activities that would hinder renewal of soul and body, e.g., needless work and business activities, unnecessary shopping, etc.

2. To lead a sacramental life: to receive Holy Communion frequently and the Sacrament of Penance regularly – minimally, to receive the Sacrament of Penance at least one a year (annu-

al confession is obligatory only if serious sin is involved).

*– minimally, to receive Holy Communion at least once a year, between the first Sunday of Lent and Trinity Sunday.

3. To study Catholic teaching in preparation for the Sacrament of Confirmation, to be confirmed, and then to continue to study and advance the cause of Christ.

4. To observe the marriage laws of the Church: * to give religious training (by example and word) to one's children; to use parish schools and religious education programs.

5. To strengthen and support the Church: * one's own parish community and parish priests; the worldwide Church and the Holy Father.

6. To do penance, including abstaining from meat and fasting from food on the appointed days. *

7. To join in the missionary spirit and apostolate of the Church.

Holy Days of Obligation in the United States

1. All Sundays of the year
2. January 1 – Solemnity of Mary, the Mother of God
3. Ascension Thursday – 40 days after Easter
4. August 15 – Assumption of the Blessed Virgin Mary
5. November 1 – All Saints' Day
6. December 8 – The Immaculate Conception
7. December 25 – Christmas Day

Fast and Abstinence

The obligation to fast allows Catholics from ages 21-59 to have one full meal and two smaller meals during a day of fast. The obligation to abstain does not allow Catholics from the age of 14 and older to eat meat on days of abstinence.

Ash Wednesday and Good Friday are days of fast and abstinence, while all Fridays during Lent are days of abstinence. The regulations concerning fast and abstinence vary from diocese to diocese.

Everyday Prayers

Sign of the Cross

In the name of the Father,
and of the Son, † and of the
Holy Spirit.
Amen.

The Lord's Prayer

Our Father, who art in heaven,
hallowed be thy name;
thy kingdom come;
thy will be done on earth as it is
in heaven.

Give us this day our daily bread;
and forgive us our trespasses
as we forgive those who trespass
against us;
and lead us not into temptation,
but deliver us from evil.
Amen.

The Hail Mary

Hail Mary, full of grace,
the Lord is with thee.
Blessed art thou among women,
and blessed is the fruit
of thy womb, Jesus.

Holy Mary, Mother of God,
pray for us sinners,
now and at the hour of our death.
Amen.

Glory Be to the Father

Glory be to the Father, and to the Son,
and to the Holy Spirit.
As it was in the beginning, is now
and ever shall be, world without end.
Amen.

Grace Before Meals

Bless us, O Lord, and these your gifts
    which we are about to receive
    from your bounty,
    through Christ our Lord.
    Amen.

Grace After Meals

We give you thanks, Almighty God,
    for these and all your blessings;
    you live and reign for ever and ever.
    Amen.

Come Holy Spirit

Come, Holy Spirit, fill the hearts
    of your faithful and
    kindle in them the fire of your love.

Send forth your Spirit,
    and they shall bc created; And you
    will renew the face of the earth.

O God,
    on the first Pentecost
    you instructed the hearts of those
    who believed in you

by the light of the Holy Spirit;
under the inspiration
of the same Spirit,
give us a taste
for what is right and true
and a continuing sense
of his presence and power;
through Jesus Christ our Lord.
Amen.

An Act of Faith

O God,
I firmly believe all the truths
that you have revealed
and that you teach us
through your Church,
for you are truth itself and
can neither deceive nor be deceived.

An Act of Hope

O God,
> I hope with complete trust that you
> will give me,
> through the merits of Jesus Christ,
> all the necessary grace in this world
> and everlasting life
> in the world to come,
> for this is what you have promised
> and you always keep your promises.

An Act of Charity

O God,
> I love you with my whole heart
> above all things,
> because you are infinitely good;
> and for your sake
> I love my neighbor
> as I love myself.

The Apostles' Creed

I believe in God, the Father almighty,
Creator of heaven and earth.

I believe in Jesus Christ, his only Son,
our Lord.
He was conceived by the power of
the Holy Spirit
and born of the Virgin Mary.
He suffered under Pontius Pilate,
was crucified, died and was buried.
He descended to the dead.
On the third day he rose again.
He ascended into heaven,
and is seated at the right hand
of the Father.
He will come again to judge
the living and the dead.

I believe in the Holy Spirit,
the holy catholic Church,
the communion of saints,
the forgiveness of sins,
the resurrection of the body,
and life everlasting.
Amen.

The Confiteor

I confess to almighty God,
and to you, my brothers and sisters,
that I have sinned
through my own fault,
in my thoughts and in my words,
in what I have done,
and in what I have failed to do;
and I ask blessed Mary, ever Virgin,
all the angels and saints,
and you, my brothers and sisters,
to pray for me to the Lord our God.

Act of Contrition

My God, I am sorry for my sins
with all my heart.

In choosing to do wrong
and failing to do good,
I have sinned against you
whom I should love above all things.

I firmly intend with your help
to sin no more, to do penance and
to avoid whatever leads me to sin.
Amen.

PRAYERS BEFORE COMMUNION

Jesus, the Bread of Life

Father in heaven,
  you have made us for yourself;
  our hearts are restless
  until they rest in you.

Fulfill this longing through Jesus
  the bread of life,
  so that we may witness to Him
  who alone satisfies the hungers
  of the human family.

By the power of your spirit
  lead us to the heavenly table
  where we may feast on the vision of
  your glory for ever and ever.
  Amen.

Prayer before Holy Communion

Come, O blessed Savior, and nourish
　　my soul with heavenly Food,
　　the Food which contains
　　every sweetness and every delight.

Come, Bread of Angels,
　　and satisfy the hunger of my soul.

Come, glowing Furnace of Charity,
　　and enkindle in my heart
　　the flame of divine love.

Come, Light of the World,
　　and enlighten the darkness
　　of my mind.

Come, King of Kings, and
　　make me obedient to Your holy will.

Come, loving Savior,
　　and make me meek and humble.

Come, Friend of the Sick,
　　and heal the infirmities of my body
　　and the weakness of my soul.

Come Good Shepherd,
　　my God and my All,
　　and take me to Yourself.

Prayer to the Virgin Mary

Mother of mercy and love,
blessed Virgin Mary,
I am poor and unworthy
and I turn to you in confidence
and love.

You stood by your Son
as he hung dying on the cross.

Stand also by me, and by all
who are offering Mass today here
and throughout the entire Church.

Help us to offer a perfect and
acceptable sacrifice in the sight of
the holy and undivided Trinity,
our most high God.
Amen.

Prayer of St. Thomas Aquinas

Almighty and ever-living God,
I approach the sacrament of your
only-begotten Son,
our Lord Jesus Christ.

I come sick to the doctor of life,
unclean to the fountain of mercy,
blind to the radiance of eternal light,

and poor and needy to the Lord of
heaven and earth.

Lord, in your great generosity,
   heal my sickness,
   wash away my defilement,
   enlighten my blindness,
   enrich my poverty,
   and clothe my nakedness.

May I receive the bread of angels,
   the King of Kings and Lord of
   Lords, with humble reverence,
   with the purity and faith,
   the repentance and love,
   and the determined purpose that
   will help to bring me to salvation.

May I receive the sacrament
   of the Lord's body and blood,
   and its reality and power.

Kind God, may I receive the body
   of your only begotten Son,
   our Lord Jesus Christ,
   born from the womb
   of the Virgin Mary, and so
   be received into his mystical body
   and numbered among his members.

Loving Father,
as on my earthly pilgrimage
I now receive your beloved Son
under the veil of a sacrament,
may I one day see him
face to face in glory,
who lives and reigns with you
for ever. Amen.

Prayer of St. Ambrose

Lord Jesus Christ,

I approach your banquet table
in fear and trembling,
for I am a sinner,
and dare not rely on my own worth
but only on your goodness and mercy.

I am defiled by many sins
in body and soul,
and by my unguarded thoughts
and words.

Gracious God of majesty and awe,
I seek your protection,
I look for your healing.

Poor troubled sinner that I am,
I appeal to you,
the fountain of all mercy.

I cannot bear your judgment,
  but I trust in your salvation.

Lord, I show my wounds to you
  and uncover my shame before you.

I know my sins are many and great,
  and they fill me with fear,
  but I hope in your mercies,
  for they cannot be numbered.

Lord Jesus Christ, eternal king,
  God and man,
  crucified for mankind,
  look upon me with mercy
  and hear my prayer,
  for I trust in you.

Have mercy on me,
  full of sorrow and sin,
  for the depth of your compassion
  never ends.
  Praise to you, saving sacrifice,
  offered on the wood of the cross
  for me and for all mankind.

Praise to the noble and precious blood,
  flowing from the wounds
  of my crucified Lord Jesus Christ
  and washing away the sins
  of the whole world.

Remember, Lord, your creature,
    whom you have redeemed
    with your blood.

I repent my sins, and
    I long to put right what I have done.

Merciful Father,
    take away all my offenses and sins;
    purify me in body and soul,
    and make me worthy to taste
    the holy of holies.

May your body and blood,
    which I intend to receive,
    although I am unworthy,
    be for me the remission of my sins,
    the washing away of my guilt,
    the end of my evil thoughts,
    and the rebirth of my better instincts.

May it incite me to do the works
    pleasing to you and profitable
    to my health in body and soul,
    and be a firm defense against
    the wiles of my enemies.
    Amen.

PRAYERS AFTER COMMUNION

Prayer to the Virgin Mary

Mary, holy virgin mother,
  I have received your Son, Jesus Christ.

With love you became his mother,
  gave birth to him, nursed him,
  and helped him grow to manhood.

With love I return him to you,
  to hold once more,
  to love with all your heart,
  and to offer to the Holy Trinity
  as our supreme act of worship
  for your honor and for the good of
  all your pilgrim brothers and sisters.

Mother, ask God to forgive my sins and
  to help me serve him more faithfully.

Keep me true to Christ until death, and
  let me come to praise him with you
  for ever and ever.
  Amen.

Prayer to our Redeemer

Jesus, may all that is you flow into me.

May your body and blood be my food
and drink.

May your passion and death be my
strength and life.

Jesus, with you by my side enough
has been given.

May the shelter I seek be the shadow
of your cross.

Let me not run from the love which
you offer, but hold me safe
from the forces of evil.

On each of my dyings shed your light
and your love.

Keep calling to me until that day
comes, when, with your saints,
I may praise you for ever. Amen.

The Anima Christi

Soul of Christ, sanctify me.

Body of Christ, save me.

Blood of Christ, inebriate me.

Water from the side of Christ, wash me.

Passion of Christ, strengthen me.

O good Jesus, hear me.

Within your wounds, hide me.

Permit me never to be separated from you.

From the malignant enemy, defend me.

In the hour of my death, call me
and bid me to come to you,
that with your Saints, I may praise you
for ever and ever. Amen.

Prayer to Jesus Christ Crucified

My good and dear Jesus,

I kneel before you
asking you most earnestly
to engrave upon my heart a deep
and lively faith, hope, and charity,
with true repentance for my sins,
and a firm resolve to make amends.

As I reflect upon your five wounds,
and dwell upon them with deep
compassion and grief,

I recall, good Jesus, the words
the prophet David spoke
long ago concerning yourself:
they have pierced my hands and feet,
they have counted all my bones!

Prayer of St. Thomas Aquinas

Lord, Father all-powerful
and ever-living God,

I thank you,
for even though I am a sinner,
your unprofitable servant,
not because of my worth but
in the kindness of your mercy,
you have fed me with the precious
body and blood of your Son,
our Lord Jesus Christ.

I pray that this holy communion
may not bring me
condemnation and punishment but
forgiveness and salvation.

May it be a helmet of faith
and a shield of good will.

May it purify me from evil ways
and put an end to my evil passions.

May it bring me charity and patience,
humility and obedience,
and growth in the power to do good.

May it be my strong defense against
all my enemies, visible and invisible,
and the perfect calming of all my evil
impulses, bodily and spiritual.

May it unite me more closely to you,
the one true God,
and lead me safely through death
to everlasting happiness with you.

And I pray that you will lead me,
a sinner, to the banquet where you,
with your Son and Holy Spirit,
are true and perfect light,
total fulfillment, everlasting joy,
gladness without end,
and perfect happiness to your saints.
Grant this through Christ our Lord.
Amen.

Act of Thanksgiving

From the depths of my heart
I thank You, Lord,
for Your infinite kindness
in coming to me.
How good You are to me!
With Your most holy Mother and
the angels, I praise Your mercy and
generosity toward me.

I thank You for nourishing my soul
with Your Sacred Body and
Precious Blood.

I will try to show my gratitude to you
in the Sacrament of Your love,
by loving obedience
to Your holy commandments,
by fidelity to my duties,
by kindness to my neighbor and
by an earnest endeavor to become
more like You in my daily conduct.

Grant that I may spend the hours
of the day gladly working with You
according to Your will.

May I not lose my enthusiasm
in serving you.

May my conversations
be occasions of charity.

May I be patient with myself
and those around me
in the day's disappointments.

May I be mindful of others
rather than myself in moments
of fatigue and illness.

May I be generous and faithful
    so that when this day is over
    I may feel that life
    is really meaningful and peaceful for
    it has been spent
    in your loving company.
    Amen.

Prayer of Self-Dedication to Jesus Christ

Lord Jesus Christ
    take all my freedom,
    my memory, my understanding,
    and my will.

All that I have and cherish
    you have given me.

I surrender it all to be guided by
    your will.

Your grace and your love
    are wealth enough for me.

Give me these, Lord Jesus,
    and I ask for nothing more.

Prayer for Love of God

O great Lord of heaven and earth,
    infinite good and majesty,
    you who have loved men so tenderly,
    how is it that you are despised by
    so many human beings?
    You have loved me
    in a special manner
    and have bestowed
    many wonderful graces on me.
    Yet I, too, have despised you
    by every sin through which
    I have turned against your law.
    I resolve this day to love you
    with my whole heart and to love
    nothing unless it can be loved in you.
    Grant me this gift of love:
    a fervent love that will make me
    reject the appeal of sinful creatures;
    a strong love that will make me
    conquer all difficulties to please you;
    a persevering love
    that will never be dissolved.
    Amen.

DEVOTIONS TO THE SACRED HEART OF JESUS

Devotions to the Sacred Heart of Jesus

St. Margaret May Alacoque was born in France in 1647 and died in 1690. Our Lord appeared to St. Margaret Mary several times during her life as a nun in the Visitation Order. In 1675, the great revelation was made to St. Margaret Mary that she, along with Father de la Colombiere, S.J., was to be the chief instrument for instituting the Feast of the Sacred Heart and for spreading devotion to the Sacred Heart throughout the world.

The Great Promise of the First Friday

All who receive Holy Communion on nine consecutive First Fridays have been blessed by Our Lord with the grace of a most wonderful promise. We should listen carefully. It is our Saviour, Himself, who speaks to us through St. Margaret Mary:

"I promise you in the unfathomable mercy of My heart that My omnipotent love will procure the grace of final penitence for all those who communicate on nine successive First Fridays of the month; they will not die in My disfavor, or without having received their sacraments, since

My divine heart will be their sure refuge in the last moments of their life."

Our Lord also told St. Margaret Mary of the following additional blessings:

1. I will give them all the graces necessary for their state of life.
2. I will establish peace in their families.
3. I will comfort them in all their afflictions.
4. I will be their secure refuge during life, and above all in death.
5. I will bestow a special blessing upon all their undertakings.
6. Sinners shall find in My heart the source and infinite ocean of mercy.
7. Tepid souls shall grow fervent.
8. Fervent souls shall quickly mount to high perfection.
9. I will bless every place where a picture of My heart shall be exposed and honored.
10. I will give to priests the gift of touching the most hardened hearts.
11. Those who shall promote this devotion shall have their names written in My heart – never to be blotted out.

Act of Reparation to the Sacred Heart of Jesus

O sweet Jesus, whose overflowing charity for men is requited by so much forgetfulness, negligence and contempt, behold us prostrate before You eager to repair by a special act of homage the cruel indifference and injuries to which Your loving heart is everywhere subject.

Mindful alas! that we ourselves have had a share in such great indignities, which we not deplore from the depth of our heart, we humbly as Your pardon and declare our readiness to atone by voluntary expiation not only for our own personal offenses but also for the sins of those, who, straying far from the path of salvation, refuse in their obstinate infidelity to follow You, their shepherd and leader, or, renouncing the vows of their baptism, have cast off the sweet yoke of Your law.

We are now resolved to expiate each and every deplorable outrage committed against You. We are determined to make amends for the manifold offenses against Christian modesty in unbecoming dress and behavior, for all the foul seductions laid to ensnare the feet of the innocent, for the frequent violation of Sundays and holidays, and the shocking blasphemies uttered against You and Your saints.

We wish also to make amends for the insults to which Your vicar on earth and Your priests are subjected, for the profanation, by conscious neglect or terrible acts of sacrilege, of the very sacrament of Your divine love; and lastly for the public crimes of nations who resist the rights and the teaching authority of the Church which You have founded.

Would, O divine Jesus, we were able to wash away such abominations with our blood! We now offer in reparation for these violations of Your divine honor, the satisfaction You did once make to Your eternal Father on the Cross and which You continue to renew daily before us; we offer it in union with the acts of atonement of Your virgin mother and all the saints and of the pious faithful on earth; and we sincerely promise to make recompense as far as we can with the help of Your grace, for all neglect of Your great love and for the sins we and others have committed in the past.

Henceforth we will live a life of unwavering faith, of purity of conduct, of perfect observance of the precepts of the Gospel and especially that of charity.

We promise to the best of our power to prevent others from offending You and to bring as many as possible to follow You.

O loving Jesus, through the intercession of the Blessed Virgin Mary, our model in reparation, deign to receive the voluntary offering we make of this act of expiation; and by the crowning gift of perseverance keep us faithful unto death in our duty and the allegiance we owe to You, so that we may all one day come to that happy home, where You with the Father and the Holy Spirit live and reign, God, world with end. Amen.

Act of Consecration of the Human Race to the Sacred Heart

Most sweet Jesus, Redeemer of the human race, look down upon us humbly prostrate before You. We are Yours, and Yours we wish to be; but to be more surely united with You, behold each one of us freely consecrates himself today to Your Most Sacred Heart. Many indeed have never known You; many too, despising Your precepts, have rejected You. Have mercy on them all, most merciful Jesus, and draw them Your Sacred Heart. Be

King, O Lord, not only of the faithful who have never forsaken You, but also of the prodigal children who have abandoned You; grant that they may quickly return to their Father's house lest they die of wretchedness and hunger. Be King of those who are deceived by erroneous opinions, or whom discord holds aloof, and call them back to the harbor of truth and unity of faith, so that soon there may be but one flock and one shepherd. Grant, O Lord, to Your Church assurance of freedom and immunity from harm; give peace and order to all nations, and make the earth resound from pole to pole with one cry: "Praise to the Divine Heart that wrought our salvation; to it be glory and honor for ever." Amen.

Litany of the Sacred Heart of Jesus

Lord, have mercy,

Christ, have mercy,

Lord, have mercy. Christ, hear us.

Christ, graciously hear us.

God the Father of heaven,
– Have mercy on us.

God the Son, Redeemer of the world.

(After each invocation, respond with,
"Have mercy on us.")

God the Holy Spirit,

Holy Trinity, one God,

Heart of Jesus, Son of the eternal Father,

Heart of Jesus, formed by the Holy Spirit
in the womb of the Virgin Mary,

Heart of Jesus,
united with God's eternal Word,

Heart of Jesus, of limitless majesty,

Heart of Jesus, temple of God among us,

Heart of Jesus, shrine of the Most High

Heart of Jesus,
house of God and gate of heaven,

Heart of Jesus, glowing with love for us,

Heart of Jesus, overflowing with
goodness and love,

Heart of Jesus, full of kindness and love,

Heart of Jesus, fountain of all holiness,

Heart of Jesus, worthy of all praise,

Heart of Jesus,
king and center of all hearts,

Heart of Jesus, treasure-house of
wisdom and knowledge,

Heart of Jesus,
    tabernacle of God's fullness,

Heart of Jesus,
    in whom the Father is well pleased,

Heart of Jesus, of whose fullness
    we have all received,

Heart of Jesus,
    desire of the everlasting hills,

Heart of Jesus, patient and full of mercy,

Heart of Jesus,
    generous to all who turn to you,

Heart of Jesus, source of life and holiness,

Heart of Jesus, atonement for our sins,

Heart of Jesus,
    overwhelmed with reproaches,

Heart of Jesus, bruised for our sins,

Heart of Jesus,
    obedient all the way to death,

Heart of Jesus, pierced with a lance,

Heart of Jesus,
    source of all consolation,

Heart of Jesus, our life and resurrection,

Heart of Jesus,
    our peace and reconciliation,

Heart of Jesus, sacrifice for sin,

Heart of Jesus,
    salvation of all who trust in you,

Heart of Jesus,
    hope of all who die in you,

Heart of Jesus, delight of all the saints,

Lamb of God, you take away
    the sins of the world,
    – Spare us, O Lord,

Lamb of God you take away
    the sins of the world,
    – Graciously hear us, O Lord.

Lamb of God, you take away the sins
    of the world, – Have mercy on us.

Jesus, gentle and humble of heart,
    – Touch our hearts and make them
    like your own.

Let us pray.

Father, rejoice in the gifts of love
    we have received from the heart of
    Jesus your Son.

Open our hearts to share his life and
    continue to bless us with his love.

We ask this through Christ our Lord.
    Amen.

THE WAY OF THE CROSS

The Way of the Cross

The Way of the Cross is a devotion in which we meditate upon the passion of Christ. Through this devotion, we can experience Jesus' suffering as he made his way to Calvary, and feel his love – a love so great that he was willing to die for both ourselves and his Father. If we can begin to understand the human experience of suffering out love for one another, we will then begin to understand the meaning of the Cross.

THE STATIONS OF THE CROSS

Opening Prayer

All-loving God, I raise my mind and heart to you in praise.

Though weak and at times sinful I wish to follow your Son, Jesus, on the way of the cross.

May this meditation enable me to imitate in my own life the love with which he gave himself to you and to all his brothers and sisters.

Amen.

FIRST STATION

Jesus is condemned to death

The high priest then stood up before the whole assembly and put this question to Jesus, "What is this evidence these men are bringing against you?" But he was silent and made no answer at all. The high priest put a second question to him, "Are you the Christ," he said "the Son of the Blessed one?" "I am," said Jesus "and you will see the Son of Man seated at the right hand of the Power and coming with the clouds of heaven." The high priest tore his robes, "What need of witnesses have we now?" he said, "You heard the blasphemy. What is your finding?" And they all gave their verdict: he deserved to die.

MK. 14, 60-64

Lord Jesus Crucified, have mercy on me.

SECOND STATION

Jesus carries his Cross

Pilate had Jesus brought out, and seated himself on the chair of judgment... "Here is your king" said Pilate to the Jews. "Take him away, take him away!" they said.

"Crucify him!" "Do you want me to crucify your king?" said Pilate. The chief priest answered, "We have no king except Caesar." So in the end Pilate handed him over to them to be crucified. They then took charge of Jesus, and carrying his own cross he went out of the city to the place of the skull or, as it was called in Hebrew, Golgotha.

JN. 19, 13-17

Lord Jesus Crucified, have mercy on me.

THIRD STATION

Jesus falls the first time

Jesus said:

"If the world hates you, remember that it hated me before you. If you belonged to the world, the world would love you as its own; but because you do not belong to the world, because my choice withdrew you from the world, therefore the world hates you. Remember the words I said to you: A servant is not greater than his master. If they persecuted me, they will persecute you too."

JN. 15, 18-20

Lord Jesus Crucified, have mercy on me.

FOURTH STATION

Jesus meets his afflicted mother

Near the cross of Jesus stood his mother and his mother's sister, Mary the wife of Clopas, and Mary of Magdala. Seeing his mother and the disciple he loved standing near her, Jesus said to his mother, "Woman, this is your son." Then to the disciple he said, "This is your mother." And from that moment the disciple made a place for her in his home.

JN. 19, 25-27

Lord Jesus Crucified, have mercy on me.

FIFTH STATION

Simon of Cyrene helps Jesus to carry his Cross

And when the soldiers had finished making fun of him, they took off the purple and dressed him in his own clothes. They led him out to crucify him. They enlisted a passerby, Simon of Cyrene, father of Alexander and Rufus, who was coming in from the country, to carry his cross. They brought Jesus to the place

called Golgotha, which means the place
of the skull.

MK.15, 20-22

Lord Jesus Crucified, have mercy on me.

SIXTH STATION

Veronica wipes the face of Jesus

The King will say to those on his right
hand, "Come, you whom my Father has
blessed, take for your heritage the kingdom
prepared for you since the foundation of the
world… The virtuous will say to him in
reply, "Lord, when did we see you hungry
and feed you; or thirsty and give you drink?
When did we see you a stranger and make
you welcome; naked and clothe you; sick or
in prison and go to see you?" And the King
will answer, "I tell you solemnly, in so far as
you did this to one of the least of these
brothers of mine, you did it to me."

MT. 25, 34, 37-40

Lord Jesus Crucified, have mercy on me.

SEVENTH STATION

Jesus falls the second time

Ours were the sufferings he bore, ours
the sorrows he carried. But we, we thought
of him as someone punished, struck by God,
and brought low. Yet he was pierced through
for our faults, crushed for our sins. On him
lies a punishment that brings us peace, and
through his wounds we are healed.

We had all gone astray like sheep, each
taking his own way, and Yahweh burdened
him with the sins of all of us.

IS. 53, 4-6

Lord Jesus Crucified, have mercy on me.

EIGHTH STATION

Jesus meets the women of Jerusalem

Large numbers of people followed him,
and of women too, who mourned and
lamented for him. But Jesus turned to
them and said, "Daughters of Jerusalem,
do not weep for me; weep rather for your-
selves and for your children."

LK. 23, 27-28

Lord Jesus Crucified, have mercy on me.

NINTH STATION

Jesus falls a third time

Jesus said,
"I have come from heaven,
not to do my own will,
but to do the will of the one who sent me.
Now the will of him who sent me
is that I should lose nothing
of all that he has given to me,
and that I should raise it up on the last day."

JN. 6, 38-39

Lord Jesus Crucified, have mercy on me.

TENTH STATION

Jesus is stripped of his clothes

They gave him wine to drink mixed with gall, which he tasted but refused to drink. When the soldiers had finished crucifying Jesus, they took his clothing and divided it into four shares, one for each soldier. His undergarment was seamless, woven in one piece from neck to hem; so they said to one another, "Instead of tearing it, let's throw dice to decide who is to have it." In this way the words of scripture were fulfilled: 'They shared out my clothing among them. They cast lots for my clothes.' This is exactly what the soldiers did.

MT. 27, 34-35

Lord Jesus Crucified, have mercy on me.

ELEVENTH STATION

Jesus is nailed to the Cross

At the place called The Skull, they crucified him there and the two criminals also, one on the right, the other on the left. Jesus said, "Father, forgive them; they do not know what they are doing"... The people stayed there watching him. As for the leaders they jeered at him. "He saved others," they said "let him save himself if he is the Christ of God, the Chosen One." The soldiers mocked him too, and when they approached to offer him vinegar they said, "If you are the King of the Jews, save yourself." Above him there was an inscription: "This is the king of the Jews."

LK. 23, 33-38

Lord Jesus Crucified, have mercy on me.

TWELFTH STATION

Jesus dies on the cross

It was now about the sixth hour and, with the sun eclipsed, a darkness came over the whole land until the ninth hour. The veil of the Temple was torn right down the middle; and when Jesus had cried out in a loud voice, he said, "Father, into your hands I commit my spirit." With these words he breathed his last.

LK. 23, 44-46

Lord Jesus Crucified, have mercy on me.

THIRTEENTH STATION

The body of Jesus is taken down from the Cross

When the soldiers came to Jesus, they found he was already dead, and so instead of breaking his legs one of the soldiers pierced his side with a lance; and immediately there came out blood and water... After this, Joseph of Arimathaea, who was a disciple of Jesus – though a secret one

because he was afraid of the Jews – asked
Pilate to let him remove the body of Jesus.
Pilate gave permission, so they came and
took it away.

JN. 19, 33-34, 38

Lord Jesus Crucified, have mercy on me.

FOURTEENTH STATION

Jesus is laid in the tomb

So Joseph took the body, wrapped it in
a clean shroud and put it in his own new
tomb which he had hewn out of the rock.
He then rolled a large stone across the
entrance of the tomb and went away.

MT. 27, 59-60

Lord Jesus Crucified, have mercy on me.

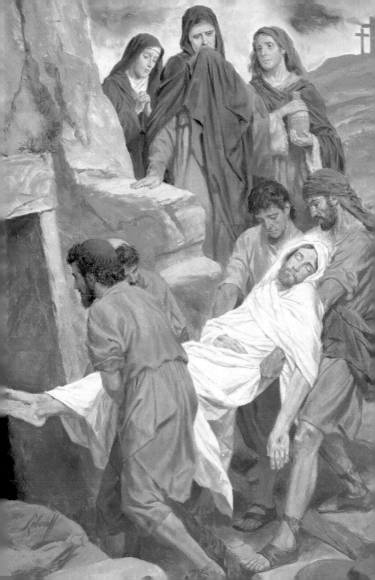

Prayers to the Blessed Virgin Mary

The Regina Caeli

"Queen of Heaven"

Queen of heaven, rejoice, Alleluia.
   The Son whom you were privileged
   to bear,
      Alleluia, has risen as he said,
   Alleluia.

Pray to God for us, Alleluia.

Rejoice and be glad, Virgin Mary,
   Alleluia.
   For the Lord has truly risen.
   Alleluia.

Let us pray. O God
   it was by the Resurrection of
   your Son,
   our Lord Jesus Christ,
   that you brought joy to the world.

Grant that through the intercession of
   the Virgin Mary, his Mother, we
   may attain the joy of eternal life.

Through Christ, our Lord. Amen.

The Angelus

The angel of the Lord declared unto
Mary.

And she conceived of the Holy Spirit.
Hail Mary…

Behold the handmaid of the Lord.

Be it done to me according to your
word. Hail Mary…

And the Word was made flesh;
and dwelt among us. Hail Mary…

Pray for us, O holy Mother of God,
that we may be made worthy
of the promises of Christ.

Let us pray.

Pour forth, we beseech You, O Lord,
your grace in our hearts, that we, to
whom the Incarnation of Christ,
Your Son, was made known
by the message of an angel,
may by his Passion and Cross
be brought to the glory of his
Resurrection; through the same
Christ our Lord.
Amen.

The Memorare

Remember, O most gracious Virgin Mary,
that never was it known that
anyone who fled to your protection,
implored your help,
or sought your intercession
was left unaided.

Inspired by this confidence, we fly unto
you, O Virgin of virgins, our Mother!

To you we come, before you we stand,
sinful and sorrowful.

O Mother of the Word incarnate,
despise not our petitions, but
in your mercy hear and answer us.
Amen.

Prayer of St. Alphonsus Liguori

O most holy and Immaculate Virgin,
my Mother; you are the Mother of
my Lord, the Queen of the world,
the advocate, hope, and refuge of
sinners, and I, the most miserable of
those sinners, come to you today.

I venerate you, great Queen, and thank
you for the many graces that you
have bestowed upon me, and I

especially want to thank you for having saved me so many times from the punishment of God, a punishment which I deserved.

I love you, most lovable Lady, and by the love I have for you, I promise that I will always serve you and do as much as I can to make others love you.

I put all of my hope and my entire salvation in you.

Receive me as your servant, O Mother of Mercy, and cover me with the mantle of your protection.

Since you are so powerful with God, free me from all temptations or, at least, obtain the graces for me to overcome them until death.

I ask of you a true love for Jesus Christ, and through you I hope to die a good death. My Mother, by the love you have for God, I beg you to always help me, especially at the last moment of my life.

Do not leave me until you see me safe in heaven.

I hope to thank and praise you there for ever.

Prayer of St. Francis de Sales

O most Holy Mary, Virgin Mother of God, even though I am most unworthy to be your servant, I moved by your motherly care for me and long to serve you.

I choose you this day to be my Queen, my Advocate and my Mother, and I firmly resolve to always be devoted to you and to do what I can to encourage others to be devoted to you.

My loving Mother, through the Precious Blood of your Son that was shed for me, I beg you to receive me as your eternal servant.

Aid me in my actions and beg for me the grace never by word, deed or thought to be displeasing in either your sight or that of your most holy Son.

Remember me, dearest Mother, and do not abandon me at the hour of my death.

Prayer of St. Louis de Montfort

Hail Mary, beloved Daughter of the eternal Father, wonderful Mother of the Son, faithful Spouse of the Holy Spirit.

You are my loving Lady, my powerful Queen.

You are all mine though your mercy, and I am all yours.

Take away everything from me that may be displeasing to God.

Cultivate in me everything that is pleasing to you.

May the light of your faith dispel the darkness of my mind, your deep humility replace my pride; your continual sight of God fill my memory with his presence; and the fire of your heart, inflame the lukewarmness of my own heart.

May your virtues take the place of my sins, and may your merits be my enrichment to make up for all that is wanting in me before God.

My beloved Mother, grant that I may
have no other spirit than yours, that
I know Jesus Christ and his Divine
Will and that I glorify the Lord.
Hail Mary, my dear Mother, may
I love God with a burning love
like yours.

Prayer of St. Thomas Aquinas

O Virgin full of goodness, the Mother
of mercy, I entrust my body and
soul, my thoughts, my actions,
and my life and death to you.

O my Queen, help me, and deliver me
from the grasp of the devil. Obtain
for me the grace of loving my Lord
Jesus Christ, your Son, with a true
and perfect love.

And after Him, O Mary, obtain for
me that same grace, so that I may
love you with all my heart and
above all things.

The Magnificat

My soul proclaims the greatness
of the Lord and my spirit
exults in God my savior;
because he has looked upon his
lowly handmaid.

Yes, from this day forward
all generations will call me blessed,
for the Almighty
has done great things for me.

Holy is his name, and his mercy reaches
from age to age
for those who fear him,

He has shown the power of his arm,
he has routed the proud of heart.

He has pulled down princes
from their thrones and
exalted the lowly.

The hungry he has filled with good
things, the rich sent empty away.

He has come to the help of Israel
his servant, mindful of his mercy –
according to the promise he made
to our ancestors – of his mercy to
Abraham and to his descendants
for ever.

MARY, MOTHER OF JESUS

Lord, make me an instrument of
    your peace.
        where there is hatred, let me sow love;
        where there is injury, pardon;
        where there is doubt, faith;
        where there is despair, hope;
        where there is darkness, light;
        and where there is sadness, joy.

O Divine Master, grant that I may not
    so much seek to be consoled as
    to console,
    to be understood as to understand,
    to be loved as to love.

For it is in giving that we receive,
    it is in pardoning
    that we are pardoned,
    and it is in dying.
    that we are born to eternal life.

                                ST. FRANCIS OF ASSISI

Litany of the Blessed Virgin Mary

Lord, have mercy,

Christ, have mercy

Lord, have mercy.

Christ, hear us.

Christ, graciously hear us.

God, the Father of heaven, have mercy
on us.

God, the Son, Redeemer of the world,
have mercy on us.

God, the Holy Spirit, have mercy on us.

Holy Trinity, one God, have mercy on us.

Holy Mary, *(after each invocation, respond
with, "Pray for us.")*

                  – Pray for us.

Holy Mother of God,

Holy Virgin of virgins,

Mother of Christ,

Mother, full of grace,

Mother most pure,

Mother most chaste,

Immaculate Mother,

Sinless Mother,

Lovable Mother,
Model of Mothers,
Mother of good counsel,
Mother of our Maker,
Mother of our Savior,
Wisest of virgins,
Holiest of virgins,
Virgin, powerful in the sight of God,
Virgin, merciful to us sinners,
Virgin, faithful to all God asks of you,
Mirror of holiness,
Seat of wisdom,
Cause of our joy,
Shrine of the Spirit,
Honor of your people,
Devoted handmaid of the Lord,
Mystical rose,
Tower of David,
Tower of ivory,
House of gold,
Ark of the covenant,
Gate of heaven,

Star of hope,

Health of the sick,

Refuge of sinners,

Comfort of the afflicted,

Help of Christians,

Queen of angels,

Queen of patriarchs,

Queen of prophets,

Queen of apostlcs,

Queen of martyrs,

Queen of confessors,

Queen of virgins,

Queen of all saints,

Queen conceived in holiness,

Quccn raised up to glory,

Queen of the rosary,

Queen of peace,

Lamb of God, you take away the sins
of the world,   – Spare us, O Lord.

Lamb of God, you take away the sins
of the world,
– Graciously hear us, O Lord.

Lamb of God, you take away the sins
of the world,   – Have mercy on us.

Pray for us, O holy Mother of God,
– That we may be made worthy
of the promises of Christ.

Let us pray.

Lord God,
give to your people the joy of
continual health in mind and body.

With the prayers of the Virgin Mary
to help us, guide us through
the sorrows of this life to
eternal happiness in the life to come.

We ask this through Christ our Lord.
Amen.

The Rosary of the Blessed Virgin Mary

"To recite the Rosary is nothing other than to contemplate the face of Christ with Mary."

Pope John Paul II

The Rosary is the most popular of all the Marian devotions. It was revealed to St. Dominic by the Blessed Mother and begun in the fifteenth century by Alen de Rupe, a Dominican preacher. The Rosary combines both vocal and meditative prayer, and is treasured by all who use it.

On October 16, 2002, Pope John Paul II published an apostolic letter titled "Rosarium Virginis Mariae." He called on Catholics to pray the Rosary and enter "the school of Mary," who knew Jesus Christ so well as his mother and his closest disciple. Though it is not mandatory, the pope suggested additions to the traditional fifteen mysteries of the Rosary. They are the Luminous Mysteries, or the Mysteries of Light, which include the mysteries of Christ's public ministry between his Baptism and his Passion. While leaving the use of these mysteries to the freedom of individuals and communities, Pope John Paul suggested that they may help to make the Rosary be a prayer centered on the life of Christ.

The complete Rosary consists of twenty decades, but is further divided into four distinct parts, each containing five decades called the Joyful, the Luminous, the Sorrowful, and the Glorious Mysteries. The Mysteries of the Rosary symbolize important events from the lives of both our Lord and the Blessed Mother. Each decade contains one mystery, an "Our Father," ten "Hail Marys," and a "Glory be to the Father." To say the Rosary, begin by making the sign of the cross and saying "The Apostles' Creed" on the crucifix, one "Our Father" on the first bead, three "Hail Marys" on the next three beads, and then a "Glory be to the Father." When this is finished, meditate upon the first mystery, say an "Our Father," ten "Hail Marys," and one "Glory be to the Father." The first decade is now completed, and to finish the Rosary proceed in the same manner until all five decades have been said.

The Five Joyful Mysteries

Mondays and Saturdays

1. The Annunciation
The Angel Gabriel tells Mary that she is to be the Mother of God.

2. The Visitation
The Blessed Virgin pays a visit to her cousin Elizabeth.

3. The Nativity
The Infant Jesus is born in a stable at Bethlehem.

4. The Presentation
The Blessed Virgin presents the Child Jesus to Simeon in the Temple.

5. The Finding in the Temple
Jesus is lost for three days, and the Blessed Mother finds him in the Temple.

The Five Luminous Mysteries

Thursdays

1. The Baptism of Jesus
Jesus is baptized in the Jordan River
by John the Baptist.

2. The Wedding at Cana
Jesus attends a wedding at Cana in
Galilee, where he turns water into wine.

3. The Proclamation of the Kingdom of God
Jesus goes through the towns and cities
of his own country proclaiming God's
Kingdom and helping the poor.

4. The Transfiguration
Jesus leads his friends up a high
mountain, where they see him
shining in glorious light.

5. The Institution of the Holy Eucharist
At supper with his friends before
he dies, Jesus gives himself to
them in bread and wine.

The Five Sorrowful Mysteries

Tuesdays and Fridays

1. The Agony in the Garden
Jesus prays in the Garden of Olives and drops of blood break through his skin.

2. The Scourging at the Pillar
Jesus is tied to a pillar and cruelly beaten with whips.

3. The Crowning with Thorns
A crown of thorns is placed upon Jesus' head.

4. The Carrying of the Cross
Jesus is made to carry his cross to Calvary.

5. The Crucifixion
Jesus is nailed to the cross, and dies for our sins.

The Five Glorious Mysteries

Wednesdays and Sundays

1. The Resurrection
Jesus rises from the dead, three days after his death.

2. The Ascension
Forty days after his death, Jesus ascends into heaven.

3. The Descent of the Holy Spirit
Ten days after the Ascension, the Holy Spirit comes to the apostles and the Blessed Mother in the form of fiery tongues.

4. The Assumption
The Blessed Virgin dies and is assumed into heaven..

5. The Crowning of the Blessed Virgin
The Blessed Virgin is crowned Queen of Heaven and Earth by Jesus, her Son.

Hail, Holy Queen

Hail, holy Queen, mother of mercy, our life, our sweetness, and our hope.

To you we cry, poor banished children of Eve; to you we send up our sighs, mourning and weeping in this valley of tears.

Turn then, O most gracious advocate, your eyes of mercy toward us, and after this our exile, show unto us the blessed fruit of your womb, Jesus.

O clement, O loving, O sweet Virgin Mary.

V. Pray for us, O holy Mother of God

R. That we may be made worthy of the promises of Christ.

Let us pray.

O God, whose only begotten Son, by his life, death and Resurrection, has purchased for us the rewards of eternal life, grant, we beseech you, that meditating upon these Mysteries of the most Holy Rosary of the Blessed Virgin Mary, we may imitate what they contain and obtain what they promise.

Through the same Christ our Lord. Amen.

Prayers to Saint Joseph

Prayer to Saint Joseph

Loving Saint Joseph, may your holy life be an inspiration to me when I find it difficult to be faithful in the fulfillment of my duties.

You are now glorified with Jesus and Mary and are a powerful intercessor at the throne of God.

Blessed foster-father of Jesus, extend to me the same tender care with which you protected Jesus and Mary that I may walk securely in the path of salvation.

Obtain for me strong faith, ardent love and zeal in doing good. With Jesus and Mary, help me at the hour of my death so that I may partake of the complete redemption of the children of God and eternally praise the Father, Son, and Holy Spirit. Amen.

Prayer to Saint Joseph, the Worker

Glorious Saint Joseph, model of all who are dedicated to labor, obtain for me the grace to work in the spirit of love and faithfully to place my responsibilities above my own desires.

Help me to work with joy and gratitude.

Let me consider it an honor to use and develop the gifts I have received from God.

Aid me to work with order, peace, moderation and patience.

Help me to work above all for the glory of God and the coming of his kingdom.

May I remember that I am to give an account of the gifts and talents I have received.

Prayer to Saint Joseph for Others

Saint Joseph, be my patron and intercessor with God.

Through the merits of Jesus and Mary obtain for me pardon of all my sins.

Implore for me a great purity of heart, a lively faith, firm hope and perfect charity.

Help me in all my needs of soul and body but most of all in the hour of my death.

Come to me then with Jesus and Mary and let me die in their love and with the help of your prayers.

Glorious Saint Joseph, powerful protector of holy Church, I implore your heavenly aid for the whole Church on earth, especially for the Holy Father and all bishops, priests and religious.

Guide and help all government officials, comfort the afflicted, console the dying, and convert sinners. Have pity on all who have died especially members of my own family and friends.

Allow them to join you and the saints in the praise and glory of God. Amen.

Prayer to Saint Joseph for Strength

Saint Joseph, we confidently invoke your patronage.

By that charity with which you were united to the Immaculate Virgin Mother of God, and by that fatherly love with which you embraced the child Jesus, we beg you and humbly pray that you will look graciously upon the inheritance which Jesus Christ purchased by his blood and assist us in our need by your power and strength.

Most watchful guardian of the holy family, protect the chosen people of Jesus Christ.

Keep far from us, most loving father, all blight of error and corruption.

Mercifully help us from heaven, most valiant defender, in this conflict with the powers of darkness. And even as of old you rescued the child Jesus from the peril of his life, so now defend God's holy Church from the snares of the enemy and from all adversity.

Keep us one and all under your continual protection, that supported by your example and your help, we may lead a holy life, die a happy death and come at last to the possession of everlasting blessedness in heaven.
Amen.

Prayer to Saint Joseph, the Guardian

O Blessed Saint Joseph, faithful guardian and protector of virgins to whom God entrusted Jesus and Mary, I implore you by the love which you did bear them, to preserve me from every defilement of soul and body, that I may always serve them in holiness and purity of love.
Amen.

Prayer to Saint Joseph

O Holy Joseph, chaste spouse of the Mother of God, most glorious advocate of all who are in danger or in their last agony, and most faithful protector of all the servants of Mary, I, in the presence of Jesus and Mary, do from this moment choose you for my powerful patron and advocate, and I implore you to obtain for me through your powerful intercession the grace of a happy death.

Receive me, therefore, as your perpetual servant, and recommend me to the constant protection of Mary, your spouse, and to the everlasting mercies of Jesus, my Savior.

Assist me in all the actions of my life, which I now offer to the greater glory of Jesus and Mary.

Never, therefore, forsake me; and whatsoever grace you see most necessary and profitable for me, obtain it for me now and also at the hour of my death.

I know not when I shall die, but whatsoever hour it shall happen I invite
you to be with me at my deathbed.

Through your gracious intercession may
there be granted me in my last hour all
the graces I need, through the merits of
Jesus Christ, my Savior, who together
with the Father and the Holy Spirit,
lives and reigns, world without end.
Amen.

Prayer to Saint Joseph

*Especially recommended to be said with the
Rosary during October*

To you, O blessed Joseph,
we have recourse in our affliction;
and having implored the help of
your most holy Spouse, we confidently invoke your patronage also.

By that charity which bound you
to the Immaculate Virgin,
Mother of God,
and by the fatherly love with
which you embraced the Child Jesus,
look down, we beseech you,
with gracious eye on the precious

inheritance which Jesus Christ
purchased in his blood,
and help us in our necessities
by your power and aid.

Protect, O most watchful guardian
of the Holy Family,
the elect children of Jesus Christ;
ward off from us,
O most loving father,
all blight of error and corruption;
aid us from on high,
O most valiant defender, in our
struggle with the powers of darkness;
and, even as of old
you rescued the Child Jesus
from the peril of his life,
so now defend God's Holy Church
from the snares of the enemy and
from all adversity.

Shield also each one of us
by your constant protection, so that,
supported by your example and
your aid, we may live a holy life,
die a happy death, and attain
everlasting happiness in heaven.
Amen.

Litany of St. Joseph

Lord, have mercy.

Christ, have mercy.

Lord, have mercy.

Christ, hear us.

Christ, graciously hear us.

God, the Father of heaven,
have mercy on us.

God, the Son, Redeemer of the world,
have mercy on us.

God the Holy Spirit, have mercy on us.

Holy Trinity, one God, have mercy on us.

Holy Mary,   – Pray for us.

St. Joseph, *After each invocation, respond
with, "Pray for us."*

Renowned descendant of David,

Light of patriarchs,

Husband of the Mother of God,

Chaste guardian of the Virgin,

Foster-father of the Son of God,

Watchful defender of Christ,

Head of the holy family,

Joseph, most just,

Joseph, most pure,

Joseph, most prudent,

Joseph, most valiant,

Joseph, most obedient,

Joseph, most faithful,

Mirror of patience,

Lover of poverty,

Model of artisans,

Glory of domestic life,

Guardian of virgins,

Mainstay of families,

Consolation of those in trouble,

Hope of the sick,

Patron of the dying,

Protector of holy Church.

Lamb of God, you take away the sins
of the world,   – Spare us, O Lord.

Lamb of God, you take away the
sins of the world
          – Graciously hear us, O Lord.

Lamb of God, you take away the sins
of the world,   – Have mercy on us.

He made him lord of his household,
  – And ruler over all his possessions.

Let us pray.

God,
  in your infinite wisdom and love
  you chose Joseph to be the husband
  of Mary, the mother of your Son.

May we have the help of his prayers
  in heaven and enjoy his protection
  on earth.

We ask this through Christ our Lord.
  Amen.